GAINING AN ANGEL

A Mother's Story of Surviving Loss and
Finding Strength in God and Herself

Jammie Fabick

Copy editing by Effrosyni Moschoudi
Cover photo of Helen Fabick and her standard poodle, Lily.

CONTENTS

Forward 5

Losing Helen...12

Back Home 17

The Lights Go Out..24

Opioids & Helen's Struggles Here on Earth .35

Close to Home 44

A Family Shattered 48

Pain 55

Having Faith 67

Healing 71

The Universe Has My Back 86

A Note on The Opioid Epidemic...................91

About the Author 99

Forward

I am Jammie Fabick, a mother of three children… Rebecca Fabick, Helen Fabick, who would be twenty-three if she were still here with us, and John Fabick IV.

Each one of us grieves losing Helen very differently, and we've all come to respect that about each other.

Because grieving is different for everyone, I don't have any easy fix or the perfect words to say about the pain you're feeling over the loss of someone dear to you. But this book comes from my heart, my experience and my journey. I can't possibly know what *you* are going through—the difficult path you continue to walk daily, but please know you are not alone.

I understand how lonely and cold loss can feel, especially when you see the whole world happily moving on around you—while you feel paralyzed and mad. I've often cried and asked, *why is the sun out? Why is there news on TV and traffic on the roads?* I felt so confused over how the world could keep spinning when I'd died inside. The lights had gone out in my heart. I felt nauseous, like an elephant sat where my heart used to be, or as if glass shards had been placed inside of me, so that every breath reminded me of Helen and my loss.

I started this book days after Helen passed away. Six years have gone by since that day, and since the first words I wrote in a journal. They were a prayer.

I felt for so long that I'd *lost* Helen, but I've come to understand that I've *gained* an Angel.

Trust me, it didn't feel like that for many years. This journey isn't easy. It is a day to day walk, sometimes at a snail's pace. Some days are like the Daytona 500 whizzing by. It's messy, and there are tears of sadness and lonely moments looking at her picture, but also laughter at her antics when she was alive.

When Helen passed, Father Steve Giljum and Bishop Rice came to my house to be with the family, offer prayer and perform a full mass for all of us. Bishop Rice said, "We should not try and figure this all out, that would just drive us crazy." He said, "You must trust God's plan and fully trust in your faith." Father Steve and Bishop Rice have been beside my family every step of this journey. Their homilies at Helen's mass were powerful and comforting. I am forever grateful for their support and their words. I reflect on those words often!

My family, broken-hearted as they were, all showed up and stood next to us to prop us up with love. Every day since then, they've been there for me. There are countless friends of Helen's who share memories of her. The sweet texts and phone calls I still receive from them buoy me. I love watching them carry *Helen-spirit* into their lives. I want to thank every one of those people for their words of comfort and prayers of strength, for showing up and being part of my healing path.

Thank you!

There are two very special healing places in St. Louis where I spent so much of my time after Helen's death. The first place is St. Clement chapel. I would go to the chapel once or twice a day during the first two years. The chapel is so peaceful. You can sit in prayer in front of the Eucharist on the altar. It was such a powerful experience; it felt so sacred. That chapel holds many of my prayers and tears. The grounds of St. Clement church and school hold years and years of memories for me. All my children attended grade school, received first communion and were confirmed into the Church there. We, as family, attended mass there for twenty-six years. We also held Helen's funeral visitation there—in the same sanctuary where I watched her sing songs in a kindergarten play, take first communion, and stand with braces to graduate eighth grade, full of excitement for the high school life that lay ahead of her.

How was her body lying in a casket just two short years later?

But the power of the chapel and its sacred safe spaces kept calling me to come, sit and soak in the nourishment of the Eucharist and the power of prayer. I could literally feel the power of the prayers of those praying around me, their words bold and full of conviction. I have no idea what they were praying for, or the words being spoken, but my heart felt it, and my entire being absorbed their strength. During these times, tears would roll down my cheeks, hot on my skin, but I would also feel some release from the pain and sadness. I felt safe and protected, my mind could rest and my heart stopped aching for a moment.

None of those people in the church have any idea how they were a part of my healing. I am so grateful and filled with gratitude for my St. Clement community of friends and parishioners who prayed alongside me and helped me start healing. St. Clement and Ursuline academy took this family under their wings and lifted us in every way. Thank you to all of you who kept us in your prayers from day one.

My second place of solace is Queeny Park. I didn't understand until recently how crucial my time walking in nature was—not until I started writing this book. Miles upon miles of walking and many beautiful sunsets helped healed me.

I had an epiphany when I reflected on the question "How did I get through these last six years?" I had to go back to the beginning, and I remembered my friends calling me and saying, "Jammie, just come walk with us, I promise it's a safe space and you can say whatever you want or not talk at all, scream, cry, but get your shoes on and come on!" My friends encouraged me every day, *literally*, every single day for five years… Even in the cold and snow, and I do *not* like the cold! But every day I had a purpose—show up and be there! It was a lifeline I had no idea could transform and heal me. They talked about their kids and their lives and it felt so good to step away from what I was dealing with, listen and *be* with these amazing women. They'd say, "see you tomorrow!" and it made me want to get up and get out and live again. Being part of this group made me feel connected again.

The hills in the park distracted me from being inside my own head and in a fog. Those hills woke up the numbness in my body! It was like, *Hello, you are still in the land of the living.* It helped me notice nature and *be* with living trees and flowers and hear others talking and laughing. These women are Angels. I am forever grateful for their love and support. That park and those women will always hold a special place in my heart.

After my daughter, Rebecca, graduated from college, she moved to Milan, Italy and I traveled a lot to visit her. We took amazing mother daughter trips to Croatia, Greece, Morocco and Switzerland. These trips also brought me back to life. It helped to bring pieces of my heart back, made me want to be alive. I have had some incredible experiences since Helen's death. Life is beautiful and each moment is precious.

Recently, Rebecca got married. It was the most fabulous event! Planning it was so much fun, and Rebecca and I shared many special moments. And all the while, Helen was right there watching over us. She sent signs in ways that Rebecca and I recognized and we would laugh and throw our hands up and say "Hey Helen!"

Rebecca's husband, Kyle, has been an absolute Godsend to us. He's been with her for ten years and he was front and center hugging, loving and encouraging us, and of course, making us laugh! Thanks to Kyle, my son Jackson has had an older brother to be there and encourage him.

I treasure my moments with Rebecca and Jax and Kyle. The three of us have gone to grief counseling together, traveled, had fights and disagreements and had a million moments filled with love, gratitude, joy and laughter. Through the years we have grown so much together. We support each other and unconditionally love and show up for each other.

My blessing is that you find truth, peace and joy through this book. Remember pain isn't here to break us, it's here to lift us up and remind us how strong we truly are. I hope this book reminds you of your strength and that when we lose loved ones, we don't really lose them.

We just gain angels.

Losing Helen

Saturday, February 8, 2014
Oxford, Mississippi

On Saturday, I awoke in our Oxford condo instead of my own bed back in Missouri. My daughter, Rebecca, had asked me to help her organize an alumni brunch to raise money for the redecoration of her sorority house, which was why I found myself three hundred and sixty-six miles from home in Mississippi. I was looking forward to a day with my eldest, and we spent the earliest part of the morning chatting about an endless array of details over coffee with her boyfriend, Kyle. Soon after, head swirling with to-do lists, Rebecca went ahead to get her brunch underway.

Kyle and I headed back to the condominium. When we got there, we began to talk about going out for breakfast when my phone rang mid-conversation. I fished in my purse for my cell, like I had a million times before. Chances were good it was Becca, calling with a forgotten detail or idea to bounce.

I answered, but heard no cheery *hello* from the opposite end of the line. Instead, I heard my husband, Doug, speaking my youngest daughter's name.

"Helen's dead. Helen's gone."

His voice was steady and flat.

Helen's dead.

I threw the phone as hard as I could. I needed to get it *away* from me, as if distance between myself and those words could stop time—*reverse* time—change everything back to the moments before I answered that call. Even as my cell struck the television screen and burst into a million pieces of plastic and glass, I knew there would be no escaping what I could *feel* was the truth.

Helen's dead.

Horror ricocheted through my body, tearing me apart from the inside. Though my mind hadn't immediately processed the meaning of Doug's call, I'd *felt* his message was true the moment he'd uttered the words.

"What is it?" asked Kyle.

"Helen's gone. Helen's dead." I parroted Doug's words, unable to say anything else.

Kyle's face grew ashen. "What? What do you mean?"

I couldn't answer him. I was frozen; bound by the visions playing in my mind. People say when you're about to die your life flashes before your eyes, but it was *Helen's* whole seventeen years flashing through mine—everything I'd ever known and everything I'd ever wanted for her—from the moment I first held her through all our future moments, time together now doomed to be forever unspent. I watched her life lived at once—past, present and future, as quick as you can imagine.

I know at that exact moment part of me went black, dead. A light blinked out, and I couldn't even see in color anymore.

Doug called back on Kyle's phone. I recognized the chime even as I heard something else. Something much louder.

I was screaming.

I continued to wail as Doug told Kyle about Helen's death—about how he'd found her in her bed, curled up under *Blankie*, her special blanket, as if sleeping peacefully, but with her flesh cold to the touch. He told him her black standard poodle, Lily, lay beside her, forever her protector. He told him how he'd known she was dead the moment he opened her door to wake her.

At least, I assume *now* that's what he told Kyle. At the time, I was in shock. I'd left my body and I don't know where I went. I was gone.

The next thing I remember, Kyle was saying we needed to pack our things. The plane would arrive in an hour to take us home. Again, words failed me.

Does home even exist anymore?

I was no help. I honestly don't remember anything after the words, *Helen's dead*. But Kyle, being the amazing angel that he is, packed and drove us to the sorority house so we could tell Rebecca her sister was dead. I lay against the window, the cool glass against my hot cheek. My screaming had stopped, replaced by sporadic racking sobs. It felt as though my insides had been scooped out and my body had been left empty, like a deep well filled with nothing but tears.

It felt as though my heart had stopped.

My Helen Jane. My beautiful girl.

Kyle went into Rebecca's sorority house to pull her out of an alumni presentation. God is amazing to have filled Kyle with the grace to perform such a

mission—to be there to hug her and give her strength after he'd been forced to handle *me*. Kyle was an Earth angel that day. God knew Rebecca and I needed him to be there.

Kyle told Rebecca the news. I heard her ask, "Is this a joke? Is this Helen doing one of her jokes?" but she could see on my face it wasn't one of her mischievous sister's pranks. I recognized on Becca the same empty stare I knew I must have had, as if a heavy veil had dropped across her features, causing her expression to fall slack and hollow. I knew she'd left her body as well, but we weren't together in whatever that lonely place was we'd both gone to. We were each trapped in our own private hell, struggling to understand our new world. A world without Helen.

Guided by Kyle, Becca slid into the backseat of the car.

"Helen will be fine. She'll be okay," she said.

She called her friends expecting *someone* to explain to her it was all a cruel joke, but with each call, she only cried harder. No one would tell her what she needed to hear: that Helen was alive and waiting for us to come home.

She wasn't. She never would be again.

BACK HOME

On the plane I balled up and cried so hard I shook. It felt as if my heart and chest had been opened wide and everything—every ounce of everything inside me—was gushing out, *everywhere*. I felt alone, I felt scared and almost childlike. I prayed for the power to disappear, to hide somewhere faraway and deep enough the darkness couldn't find me. Rebecca and Kyle were there with me on the flight home, lost in their own pain. I'd never felt agony like that before. My whole body felt like an open wound exposed to air and salt.

Two hours later, exhausted and numb, I stepped off the plane. Family picked us up and drove us to the house where, hours before, my husband had found our daughter, dead. My world had become surreal. I moved from the plane to the car, from the car to my home like a robot, my body doing the things it was supposed to, but I don't know how. My close friends, who were standing in the driveway, appeared like a ray of light to me. I welcomed their arms around me and their heartfelt words. It was if they were holding me up with their love. Somehow, I found the tears to cry again. It was cold and they were bundled up, but I stood with no coat and no scarf—exposed to the wind and cold as if I wanted the elements to punish me for allowing my daughter to die. I'm forever grateful my friends were there waiting to walk me inside the house.

I held my son, Jackson, who'd gone through more in the previous twelve hours than any eleven year-old should ever have to experience. Doug had done his best to shield him. Knowing our Helen was lost, he'd called his cousin to come to the house to  keep Jackson occupied and away from Helen's room downstairs. Jackson still remembers the police flying into the house and asking if he had a seventeen year-old sister. He'd sent them downstairs. After that, Cousin Caren had arrived to assure him everything would be okay.

Later, Doug came upstairs and told him his sister had passed, but at his age, I don't think he fully understood.

Though part of me wished I could have been there for Jackson, I think there was a reason I was hundreds of miles away in Mississippi when she passed. I can't imagine watching my child carried out in a body bag. The neighbors saw everything and I found out later social media had exploded with the news. *Something's going down at the Fabick house.* They saw the body carried out and knew someone had died. The circus was well underway, but I was blessedly unreachable.

It was probably a good thing my phone lay mashed into bits on the floor of the condo. People talk about how they dread phone calls in the middle of the night, but I can tell you, sunlight doesn't make them any easier.

By the time I returned home, many people had gathered inside my house. They watched me move through the rooms, no one sure how to talk to me. Something about those haunted eyes watching me shifted me out of my shock and into a new mode.

I have to take care of these people. I'm the hostess. They're grieving.

I felt no less empty than I had leaning against the wall of the plane staring through the window, but habit took over and I couldn't do anything but trail along, pulled by decades of expectations. My being had split in two. Half of me had fallen into a familiar role: hostess in my own home, operating in a world where my Helen still lived, a place where I could walk around a corner and bump into her stealing a snack from a tray of hors d'oeuvres. Half of me remained a shell, an empty husk tumbling through the darkness of a world where Helen was gone. Playing hostess kept me from dealing with both halves.

It was hard enough to face people upon my return. I was never granted a moment alone where

I could go off and freak out, to grieve with my husband. We never found a moment where it could be just us, where we could cling to each other and share the terrible weight of our loss. There were just too many people. It felt like everyone I'd ever known had shown up.

Everyone, that is, but the one person I wanted to see most. Helen had been removed from the house before I returned.

I wished I could have held her before the undertaker took her. I *needed* to hug her one more time before they tore my baby apart. My logical mind knew they would have to do a complete autopsy. She was seventeen and dead. Nothing about her death made sense and it would be their job to look for evidence in her brain, her heart, her body.

I never would be able to hold her one last time the way Doug had. He'd tried to give her CPR while awaiting the paramedics. *He'd* been there with her, with her body full and intact, so from the moment I arrived home, *I* lobbied in vain for the same opportunity.

"Doug, don't let them take her out of the house," I begged, knowing she was already out of my reach. I couldn't stop asking. When he repeated she was gone, I tried a different tack.

"Call the funeral home and ask if I can go see her."

He did, but still I was denied. They told him, and then me, when I snatched the phone demanding to talk to them, it wasn't a good idea.

"No, Mrs. Fabick, you don't need to see her like this."

The process of turning my child into a collection of parts had already begun.

I had to wait for them to put my baby back together again.

Later that evening, my family arrived from Alabama and Georgia—my mother, father, sister and brother, my cousin Kama, nieces, nephews. All were eager to lend what support they could and I was happy to fall into their loving arms. For stolen moments, with them, I felt safe and warm.

Sadly, they couldn't change the pain of my new reality in any permanent way. Time and time again, I noticed my own devastation reflected in their eyes. My mother, Helen's grandmother, was a shell of her usual self. We'd both been ripped apart from the inside out. She was my mother who had given birth to me and I had given birth to Helen...she felt her own pain *and* mine. She longed to see Helen come bouncing down the stairs to ask for some of her famous Ga Ga Doris pancakes!

But we would never hear that voice again.

We moved around each other with tears at the corner of our eyes and broken hearts.

Doug and I tried to find some moments to ourselves to hold each other. We had no idea how to help each other at the time. I look back and am so sorry we didn't just lock ourselves away and cry, alone, away from all the chaos. We both went into action mode, handling details to distract ourselves from the horror. I know it sounds uncaring, but we were in shock and disbelief. Doug had *found* our baby girl...How was he functioning? He had administered CPR until the paramedics came, while the 911 caller stayed on the phone with him—this father, trying desperately to breathe life back into our daughter.

I busied myself tending for the people in my house, breaking only to go to the funeral home to see Helen for the first time since she'd peppered me with questions the day I'd flown to help Becca. I'd left my daughter alive and consumed with the details of readying herself for the Ursuline Academy high school father-daughter dance.

"Mom, did you make my hair appointment? Mom, did you make my makeup appointment? Did you press my dress? What time do I have to be there?"

I'd laid out her outfit and given her times for makeup and hair. Earlier, on the night she died, she'd sent me pictures of her spray tan—the last picture I'd ever have of her, sitting in her bed, asking me if her color looked good. The last time I talked to her had been between twelve and twelve-thirty that night and she'd been chattering about how she had to ride her horse, Moonshine, the next morning.

How could someone with so many plans just *die?*

As my first day back wore on, information about the night she died began to trickle in. The last person to talk to her was my nephew, around one-thirty a.m. They talked all the time, and he told me later they'd enjoyed the usual banter, *what's going on*, etcetera. *She'd been gossiping with her cousin moments before she died.* The coroner's report said she died around one-forty.

How is that possible?

The last person to physically see her was her brother Jackson, who talked to her in the kitchen when she came to steal his bowl of Fruit Loops. The timing was odd to me, because Jax is *not* a late-nighter. Even when he was little, he'd fall asleep at eight. For him to be in the kitchen at nearly midnight was strange. It's almost as if he knew he needed to steal those last few moments with his big sister.

Jackson said Helen told him a secret that night asking him not to tell.

He has yet to tell anyone.

THE LIGHTS GO OUT

The next time I saw Helen, she was on a gurney. I don't think seeing your child's body on a metal bed is something any parent can ever get over. I'd kissed her goodbye, busy, busy, busy, and next thing, she was lying there, lifeless.

At the funeral home, my sister, my cousin, the undertaker and I clumped into an old elevator headed to the basement of the funeral home to see Helen. Funeral homes are creepy anyway—the dark elevator and the low-ceilinged basement worked to compound my uneasiness. I felt as if I was in a CSI-type television show. Helen's head rested on one of those metal things you see on every crime show but never dream you'll see in real life. Like the bodies on television, she lay beneath a sheet.

I took one look at her hair and lost my *mind*.

Helen's naturally curly hair flopped poker straight on either side of her head. My focus locked on it with laser-like intensity. I think my brain had found a way to compartmentalize my pain. It was all too much, so when my mind threatened to overload, a little voice in my head said, *focus on her hair.*

"What have they done?" I asked, my voice

growing screechy.

The funeral director, standing in his somber suit, tried to explain to me how the embalming practice had caused her hair to straighten. He described the process in detail.

Please shut up.

I'm sure my tone had demanded an answer, but some questions aren't *really* meant to be answered in *detail*. I stood there, with that awful funeral man explaining what the other awful undertaker had done to my daughter's body.

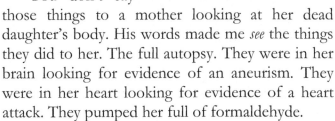

Really?!

You don't say those things to a mother looking at her dead daughter's body. His words made me *see* the things they did to her. The full autopsy. They were in her brain looking for evidence of an aneurism. They were in her heart looking for evidence of a heart attack. They pumped her full of formaldehyde.

They butchered my child's body.

I still haven't forgiven him for giving me those thoughts.

Even as they assured me her hair would be

rewashed and the curl would return, it was too late. I was crying again, half of me wailing with pain and frustration, half of me watching the broken me from somewhere above, wondering, *how can anyone survive seeing their child like that? How is this woman going to survive?*

To this day, I can't connect the dots about what my body was feeling as I looked at her lying there on a cold metal gurney with a sheet over her. I'd given birth to her. The nurses handed her tiny warm body, all five pounds, thirteen ounces of her, to *me*. I watched her take her first breath, saw her eyes open, heard her first little muffled cry.

I gave her life. Technically, I suppose it was her dad and me, but *I birthed her*. Her precious little fingers and pink, soft, tiny peanut toes.

She had the scrawniest bird legs.

For seventeen years, I was there for every milestone. Her fist steps, her first day of kindergarten, her first trip to the dentist, her first dance. It's something sacred now to look back and visit each moment of her life, both tiny and big. God gave us this incredible tiny beautiful baby. She grew in front of our eyes every day, and I still draw immense joy from those thoughts.

But at that moment, in the funeral home basement, looking at Helen's lifeless body, there was no way for me to focus on thoughts like those. I wanted her home where I could hug her. I wanted to kiss her forehead in the special spot where her little baby hair used to curl in such a unique way. I'd kissed her in that perfect spot a million times and I couldn't anymore.

Each one of my kids has their special smell. A mix of shampoo and *their* smell. I wanted to hold her one last time to capture that sensory memory, but seeing her *there*, I couldn't imagine hugging her. She was cold and not Helen anymore. The perfect baby curls were gone. Her smell was gone. I couldn't take her in my arms and make her better, the way my hugs and kisses did when she was little. I couldn't scratch her back, the way she'd begged me to her whole life.

"Mom, please come lay with me and talk and scratch my back…"

Even her hands weren't *her* hands anymore. The freckles splashed across her cheeks weren't hers anymore. I couldn't see those sparkly sapphire eyes. When Helen told a story she spoke with her eyes. There was always so much feeling in them when she talked to you—her whole body came to life. Expressive in her hand gestures, a smile that lit up the room—and if she was mad, you had to run and hide, because it was like waking a dragon. Then, her eyes would flash and her words would spit like fire. But ten minutes later, peaceful tranquil Helen would reappear as if nothing had happened.

To see her lifeless, to see that theatrical body lying so still, like a puppet whose strings had been dropped, was more than my heart and brain could bear. I felt gut-wrenching pain, nausea, numbness.

My blood seemed to leave my body. Even now, my brain won't allow me to wrap my head around what I was feeling. Maybe in ten years, but not now. No parent should have to go through that.

All at once, the lights in the basement went out.

We froze, all of us, standing there.

"This never happens," said the funeral director, his tone apologetic as he moved away to find the breaker. We could hear him scrounging around in the back.

We wiped tears, sniffling...and then burst out laughing! It was just *so Helen!* She *hated* people staring at her.

"Why is everyone looking at me? Don't look at me," was a familiar Helen-ism.

And there we were. For shame! *Staring at her.*

Take out the lights, she must have thought.

That'll stop them from staring at me.

That's how Helen made me laugh during the most horrific moment of my life.

Even dead, she found a way to make us laugh.

That was the moment I knew, in some way, she was still alive.

When the power returned, I saw Helen's body in a *new* light. That wasn't my Helen. I knew that now. I could *feel* it was just her physical body lying there. She'd always been a thousand miles an hour.

How could that still, cold shell be her?

It couldn't be. It was that simple.

The lights going out gave me comfort and propelled me through the rest of that horrible day. I found the strength to pick out a casket with Rebecca and set my mind on the details.

"She doesn't like itchy. She doesn't like satiny stuff. She's going to want soft white…"

As I looked at the different styles I tried to imagine which Helen would choose, while still wondering, *does any of this make a difference?*

Doug found his own way to disconnect from the process. He and his father began planning his father's whole funeral.

"Hey, Dad, while you're out here, why don't we pick out a casket?"

So bizarre.

Part of me thought I should be angry, but I couldn't find the fire to fight. Instead, I found my attention drawn to a casket with carved guardian angels on each of the four corners. Little Archangel Michaels to protect her at all sides.

Granted, *St. Francis* was Helen's patron saint. The girl loved animals, and she was born on October fourth, St Francis' feast day. St Francis' prayer still makes me cry every time I hear it:

Lord make me an instrument of your peace
Where there is hatred let me sow love
Where there is injury, pardon
Where there is doubt, faith
Where there is despair, hope
Where there is darkness, light

And where there is sadness, joy
O divine master grant that I may
not so much seek to be consoled as to console
to be understood as to understand
To be loved as to love
For it is in giving that we receive
it is in pardoning that we are pardoned
And it's in dying that we are born to eternal life
Amen

But there were no St. Francis caskets, and something about having St. Michael there to watch her from every corner felt right. I thanked and praised God and the angels for protecting me and *all* parents who'd lost a child. It was comforting to know Archangel Michael would walk beside me and Helen, side-by-side, every day. He'd draw his sword against anything negative trying to get near me, and he'd shield me with his golden shield.

Thank you, Archangel Michael. Thank you to all my guardian angels for protecting me and guiding me and helping me put one foot in front of the other to get this far to write all of this and share my experience.

The angels' wings have so much strength to carry us, but are also soft to comfort us. It's not possible to walk through the loss of losing a child alone. No human has that kind of strength.

It was only with divine help that I made it through the funeral. The visitation was private but five hundred people showed up. Rebecca's friends had made picture boards and images of Helen smiled from every corner. Two thousand attended the funeral at the Cathedral Basilica in St. Louis—that is a *big* crowd for a seventeen-year-old. The Cathedral is vast and has a *very* long aisle, down which we filed, walking behind her casket as they wheeled her down towards the altar. Doug and I walked together holding hands with Jackson between us. Rebecca and Kyle were with us, also holding hands. I could hear sniffles and muffled sobs as we walked past each and every pew.

Their pain stabbed at my own. It felt like stings from bees.

My hair was perfectly in place and my clothes were perfectly pressed. From the outside, I looked put together and poised.

Boy, was *that* a false façade.

I felt hollow and bare, like every nerve was exposed to the raw cold.

That event is largely a blur in my memory. I only remember bits of it. The executives from my husband's mother company walked in with their perfect suits and security details, and I rolled my eyes, thinking the pomp was all for show, but one of the men had lost a child himself and he turned out to be really sweet. His daughter had died in her sleep too, and as he shared that with Doug and me, I felt the connection. I had no handbook for how to deal with my pain, and I could tell he, too, struggled to find the words for us, because he'd had the same heart-breaking experience. I was so grateful for this man's vulnerability—his grace to share his pain with us.

Most importantly, he'd lost a child and *he was still standing*. I was in awe. It was almost an *honor* to meet someone who'd survived this kind of pain.

Years later, after meeting many more parents who'd lost children in many different ways, I realized it always feels strangely comforting to be with people who have similarly suffered. They understood if I was erratic and crying one second and desperate to be alone the next. There was no judgement involved, and I was allowed the space I needed to be supported. Each parent had a different experience, but we were all connected by one shiny golden thread from Heaven.

Through all the services on the day of the funeral, I heard the words people said to me, but their meanings were lost. I only heard a low buzzing in my head. I don't think I blinked. I don't know how my body kept upright, because my muscles felt deflated. I had to force myself to breathe.

How could I be present in that horrible new reality? How could I hear the words, "Helen is dead, she's gone" and even comprehend them? In five seconds, through a phone call, my heart, mind, spirit, logical thinking feeling, hearing—all had been torn away from me.

God and the angels step in.

There were so many people at my house after the funeral; family, friends—not to mention caterers and random others. No one could *really* look at me. They'd steal a glance at me and see my pain and sadness, and I'm sure it frightened them. They tried. They were all very sincere and warm, but they didn't know what to say. I wouldn't have known either.

Helen, whenever I am at the church I still see you in the casket. That is very hard for me. Were you happy with the outfit I chose for you? I was able to kiss your on the forehead a million times during the wake. I wanted to hold you and hug you before they took you from the house. I am sorry I wasn't here the day you passed away.

Back at the house, after the services, everyone produced pictures and told stories and laughed recalling Helen's antics. The house was full of love and seeing how much she'd meant to so many people helped me with my own pain. All those people circling around me with their support helped.

I still couldn't go downstairs to the part of the house where she died, but her friends went down. They'd *always* hung out in Helen's room, so it felt natural for them to be down there. They brought up *Blankie* for me, Helen's special blanket, and later I would walk around the house with it wrapped around me.

It *smelled* like her.

The day a parent loses a child their life is forever divided into two timeframes—life before and life after—and life after felt like a terrible nightmare. I remember watching everyone around me as if I were in a vacuum, sealed in some kind of bubble, separated from the world. It was as if there was no air moving around me, as if the Earth had stopped rotating and everything, down to tiniest sand particles and bits of dust, was completely still and quiet.

After the funeral, we packed up and left for our house in Palm Beach. I remember walking out of our Missouri house, the home that didn't feel the same anymore. The picture boards of Helen still sat on easels in the great room, the flower blanket of roses that had stretched across her casket now lay down the center of our dining room table. Cards of sympathy filled baskets on the counter. There were remnants of guests' and gatherers dishes and belongings strewn about. Walking out that door, I had no idea how I was going to return without Helen.

OPIOIDS & HELEN'S STRUGGLES HERE ON EARTH

Shortly after the funeral, we finally received the results of the autopsy and discovered the cause of Helen's death.

Opioids.

I'd seen reports about the opioid epidemic, but never dreamed it would touch my family.

How could it be?

They told me Helen had taken pills—a combination of hydrocodone, oxycodone and a little Xanax—that caused her to relax so deeply she simply didn't take her next breath.

Where had she gotten these drugs? Why? Why would she have taken enough to kill herself?

Trying to make sense of it all, we asked a doctor friend of ours to read her report. He said it wasn't the amounts—there weren't enough drugs in her system to kill her. It was the way they'd mixed.

That made a little more sense. Helen had always been sensitive to medications. A year before her death, she'd taken Solodyn for an acne break out and it had caused her brain to swell. It wasn't a common reaction. She'd needed a spinal tap to have fluid drained—all because of a drug other people took every day without problem.

The police investigating her death couldn't find anything in her room except Zoloft, for which she had a prescription.

The revelation that my child had been collecting drugs and might have used them to kill herself sent me reeling all over again.

Guide me, Helen. Enter me and show me what happened after 1:48 am. The time that you went to sleep and the angels and Jesus took you from this world. Would you like me to lay in your bed and be close to the place you took your last breath? Now I have so many questions, Helen. Now that I know your cause of death. I honestly believe you are happier. I am sorry none of us could fully understand why life here on Earth was so hard for you. Maybe I was too close to you to see. I believed in you every day.

I had to know more. I couldn't believe my Helen, so full of life, could have killed herself. Not when she'd been making so many plans. It simply wasn't possible.

When an officer returned to the house for a follow up, I begged her to tell me if she thought Helen had committed suicide.

She said, *no.*

She told me when people kill themselves the scene is always more violent—covers thrown off, signs of thrashing or anger, but there were no signs like that in Helen's case. Doug had found her looking like a sleeping angel.

To be safe, we had a drug dog sniff the house to make sure there wasn't anything stashed. Part of me hoped we'd find something to give us more information about what she was taking and from where it might have come. It was too late to save her, but I wanted to know *everything.* I wanted to *understand.*

The more I thought about the drugs they'd found in my baby's blood, the more I realize I hadn't been *completely* taken by surprise. I'd been shocked by the vilified word *opioid.* I'd been surprised by the number of different drugs in her system and that she'd been able to buy them all somewhere.

But in my quiet moments, when there was nothing but brutal honesty to keep me company, I knew we'd all had our suspicions about Helen. We knew she sometimes drank with friends, but Doug and I thought it ended there. Never in my wildest imagination had I ever considered she might be taking pills.

I look back now and realize she had an

addiction problem.

Why did you take the pills? What freak out happened? I feel you had a freak out... I wish every day you hadn't taken the pills, Helen. You would still be here had you just talked to someone that night. Jackson says you told him secrets... what are they?

Helen Jane's death wasn't the first time she'd been pulled away from me. She'd been born six weeks early on October fourth, nineteen-ninety-six. I was sick with preeclampsia; my blood pressure was through the roof and then some. She was too tiny at five pounds thirteen ounces, and they rushed her to the NICU immediately after birth to be placed in an enclosed incubator. The doctors connected her to heart and lung monitors to be sure her lungs were clean and strong. She remained there, away from me, for a little over a day.

I couldn't move. Between the medications for my blood pressure and giving birth, I could do little more than lay on my back and be very still. Only Doug could visit Helen, but even he couldn't hold her.

I remained in the intensive care unit until my blood pressure fell into a safe range, at which point they moved me into a private room where I finally held Helen for the first time. I can still see the cartoonishly large alarm sensor wrapped around her little bird leg. I'm certain it weighed more than she did. They had her few sprigs of hair in a bow. It took my breath away how beautiful and precious she was. There's no greater gift than a baby, and what a gift Helen was to all of us! I adored her beyond words. Even so tiny, her blue eyes danced with mischief.

Helen was a blessing I can't even begin to explain. She could make me so mad, and then I would look at her smile and those freckles and those blue eyes and *melt*. We had a soul connection. We were so much alike, and also so different.

The thing I miss the most is her energy. With Helen, every day was exciting.

"Let's do something. We're going to do something fun."

I miss hearing about her day. When we spent those days together, I became a part of her story. We rode horses together. She rode beautifully and competed in hunter-jumper. I'd help her tack up.

Though she was the youngest in her closest group of friends, they repeatedly did what she asked. They've told me individually they look back and think, *Why did we let her boss us around? Why did we listen to her?*

I'm sure it was her energy. She was an undeniable force.

Every day I got to spend with Helen was exciting. She could be draining—she challenged me. Sometimes she mentally drained me. She was a sensitive, loving and caring being who tried to create a protective shell of *I don't need you or anyone else*.

She could be demanding, but I knew where that came from. We were *so much alike*. I can be fiery. One time I got so mad I threw Raman noodles at her. We sometimes screamed at each other like that, and five minutes later we'd go get ice cream. Her dad would get so angry at her— he'd look at me and say, "She's just like you!"

I'd want to pull her hair out one minute and I'd be mesmerized by how precious she was the next. She was a perfectionist with herself and everybody else, but she encouraged people to be *proud* of who they were. Again and again, I heard from her friends, "Helen accepted me for me." She wanted everyone to live their lives on their own terms.

Helen always pushed things to the pins. She lived a whole lot of life in seventeen years.

There's probably a reason she didn't live very long.

But for every exhausting moment there were ten beautiful, exciting adventures. She was funny. People were drawn to her and they loved to spend time with her.

But Helen didn't spend all her time bossing around her friends. She was also very spiritual. I think she had some clairvoyance in her for sure. She would draw pictures of things she saw in church that only she could see. She was an amazing artist.

I think now how lucky I am to have been her mother. I was blessed to be chosen to be parent to that angel on Earth. I believe she was sent for a reason—to deliver a message. To save others from her fate.

Copied by Helen Jane Fabick *October 4, 1996 - February 8, 2014*

Psalm 139 – The Road Ahead:

Lord, you are the one who truly knows me. You know what lies within my heart and should. You know my every thought and word. Every feeling and emotion. You walk before me and behind me. Protecting me in an everlasting devotion Where can I hide from your light? Anywhere and everywhere do you shine? In the pure joy of my life you remain, whether in dark or light you guide me, holding my hand fast in your own. If I ever try to hide from you in the darkest of the night, your light will still shine on me for the dark is day to you.

Even with all those gifts and all that beauty, Helen had her struggles. In January, the year she died, she cut herself. She said she fell skateboarding at a friend's house, but Doug took her to the emergency room and both he and the nurses noticed cuts across her arms in perfectly straight lines.

"You didn't fall on a skateboard," said the doctor. "What's the real story?"

It took her a little time, but she eventually

admitted she'd cut herself.

By then I'd arrived and I took Doug aside.

"We need to check her in to the psych ward until we can figure out what to do. Just for two days. I don't want her to hurt herself again."

We knew Helen suffered from serious anxiety, piling pressure on herself at every opportunity. She encouraged everyone else to be comfortable in their own skin, but wasn't comfortable in her own. She'd been to a child psychiatrist before. Her perfectionism worked in her favor in many ways— she was super organized, earned straight As, was an honor student and accomplished equestrian— but she'd been diagnosed with OCD and prescribed Zoloft. She also suffered from social anxiety. She couldn't get out of her own head.

Doug and I didn't like the idea of our little girl in the psychiatric ward, but we had to debate the possibility.

Would it be better for her there?

Helen overheard our discussion and exploded at the idea. We went back and forth until we finally decided *not* to check her in. She didn't seem in immediate danger. We knew she didn't *want* to die. I remembered being a teenager, and I'd gone through some of the same tribulations. Half of me wanted to lock her up in a safe place, and half felt as though her troubles were just part of growing up.

We told ourselves we'd take her to Tucson for a dual diagnosis to help her with her depression and anxiety, as well as what we thought might be a burgeoning drinking problem. We knew she'd been drinking, and whether it was youthful folly or a form of self-medication, we wanted it addressed. Both sides of the family had experienced problems with alcoholism, so it didn't seem *odd*.

We never imagined she could also be taking pills. But the same dogged determination that earned her perfect grades in school could be turned on less desirable projects. We found out later she'd researched drugs as if she were writing a school paper. She knew it was easy for kids to find anything—OxyContin, Xanax, Adderall. Kids sold them at school. Like a detective, she hunted down someone who offered her Klonopin, with promises it would calm down her mind.

We never finished our plans for Tucson. Life got in the way, and a month later, she was dead.

What if we had checked her in? Would that have changed February eighth?

Following her death, every day, I ran through my litany of 'what ifs.'

Why couldn't you tell me what was going on?

I'd told my girls about my own teenage years and the troubles I'd gone through, and still she hadn't come to me before turning to self-medication.

What could I have done? What should I have done?

CLOSE TO HOME

After Helen died, new facts began to bubble to the surface. Her friends came forward with information. They told each other things. They knew things—things I didn't know. That she had trusted her friends with things she hadn't told me was a fresh new hell for me, something else to torture myself with in my darkest moments.

One friend told us Helen had bought drugs off the street from a dealer. The image of my child buying drugs on a corner or dark alley was terrifying, but it quickly paled against the horror of the next tale. Another friend told us where Helen received most of her drugs.

From a landscaper on our property.

Suddenly, we realized the truth. Things that had happened shortly after Helen's death appeared in a new light. Our groundskeeper had come to our house after the funeral to say he planned to kill himself. For years, he'd taken care of our grounds and pool, as well as Doug's parents' place next door. He was always around. Why would he suddenly collapse sobbing in our front yard?

My husband talked him out of killing himself and sent him home.

After his meltdown, he stopped coming to

work. He never said why.

But now, thanks to Helen's friend, we knew.

He was the one who'd given Helen the pills that killed her.

He'd gained her trust and then betrayed her in so many ways.

Helen, I will pray for God to bestow peace upon me about why you couldn't tell me the truth. I feel your pain. He was an awful, evil man. He took advantage of your innocence... Why couldn't you tell me? We didn't protect you enough. Your dad and I were stupid, and every day I will regret we weren't stronger for you.

I was still reeling with the death of my daughter. To find out she'd been abused and betrayed by a person so close to the family...that she hadn't told me...that I hadn't sensed it somehow and been there for her...

It was nearly more than I could bear.

We went to the town and country police and gave them all the information we were able to gather, but they said they couldn't prove anything. Their only witness, Helen, was dead. Her friend's stories were hearsay.

There would be no justice for that terrible man. The man who hurt my daughter. The man who had taken her to the edge with his drugs and then pushed her over.

We scrambled to find another way to make him pay. We tried to plan a sting operation but nothing ever came of it. We filed a restraining order against him. I didn't want him near me, or my family.

I saw him once more after discovering what he'd done. He came toward me on the street and I called the police. He was gone by the time they'd arrived.

Helen, why couldn't you tell me?

That man was at our house every day, a constant source of stress and shame for her. Add that to the usual anxiety that accompanies being a teenage girl and it had all been too much. She used his drugs to make herself sleep. She hadn't killed herself, but she'd tried to escape, if only for a little while.

There's something going on inside me that I can't put to words. But I feel so safe and so loved and so peaceful tonight. I just want to sit and pray for Helen. I want to just talk to the Holy Spirit about her. Helen, I know you are doing amazing things from Heaven and doing God's work every day. You love us and I know you miss us like we miss you. Do you remember last year at Christmas? The part that is painful for me to remember is that you were in so much pain and you were hiding a secret. That is so hard for me right now. That's where my heartache is. I hate to think my baby girl was in so much pain and that I didn't know everything.

How did I not know? Why didn't she tell me the truth? Why did her friends not say until it was too late?

Now, with my nieces and other kids, I tell them, *talk to people*. Let them know.

It can save a life.

A FAMILY SHATTERED

There's life before Helen's death and after. That event changed my life forever, not just by Helen's absence, but I feel as though my very DNA changed. It changed how I view people and relationships.

Through it all, Doug and I never found time to sit. I wonder now if we just *couldn't*. Looking back, I realize we didn't spend time together. There were always people around. And if you'd asked me who the first person I wanted to seek out once arriving home was—other than Helen—I couldn't tell you. I couldn't say what I wanted to do when I got off the plane. I came home and the crowd herded me. People wanted to talk to me and Doug, and I fell into my role, part of which was a *I'll just handle this on my own* attitude.

It was all too much. Soon, our marriage was over.

My Beautiful Helen,

No one understands me like you do. No one loves me like you do. You and I were two peas in a pod. You are way smarter and braver, though. I feel lonely even when I am with everyone. Your heart was so kind and good. You tried to have a tough exterior, but you were so loving inside. Your heart was so pure, Helen. You were capable of feeling. You wanted relationships. People loved everything about you. You inspired so many people. Still, to this day, you inspire them. You certainly inspire me.

I know you are right here, right beside me. I want to hug you and talk about what's happening. I am sorry if I disappointed you, Helen. I am sorry I wasn't lying next to you when you passed away. Are you mad? Did you not want me to go to Oxford? I was coming home Sunday. I want every moment back from the time you went to school on Friday. I want to have a redo. Why can't we go back? Why did you have to leave this world? When will you tell me why? I wish I knew why God took you so early. Why does he think I am strong enough to live without you? I know God, Jesus, Mary and all the angels love you…but I do, too. We were going to live together later in life. We were going to have our barn. We were going to have all the animals.

Doug and I had very different processes. After Helen's death, I prayed that God could heal our hearts, but we drifted apart.

Looking back, I know our separation had already been approaching, even without the stress and horror of Helen's death. We suffered the ebbs and flows of married life. We'd travel together and be happy, but we'd come back to every-day life raising the children and before long things would feel strained once more. Kids are difficult. *Especially* Helen has been. I'd never say she was this perfect peachy teenager—both my girls pushed their limits.

It could have been a thousand things that finally ended Doug and me. Many couples fall apart after losing a child. I wasn't there when he found Helen, and I can't imagine how that experience tore at him.

When we were in Palm Beach and it was time to take Jackson back to St. Louis for school, I flew with my son alone. Doug announced he would be staying in Florida. I was incredulous. I was hurt.

You're going to make us go home alone? Be in that house alone?

I knew it was over. Honestly, at that moment I completely let go of any belief that Doug would ever be there to comfort me or hold my hand.

Boarding the plane to fly back home to that sad, cold house was

brutal.

We'd gone to Palm Beach to get away from everything, and I was hoping I would able to sleep there. Instead, I got no sleep, and definitely not any sort of peace. Jackson had missed two weeks of school and we needed to get back.

Get back to *what*, I wasn't sure.

The anticipation of a flight without Helen's father, heading back to the house where she died, and burdened with the deep sense that Doug was gone forever, took away whatever shred of hope I had left. 'Hope' fell, blasted into a million pieces, to lay alongside my already broken heart.

My other daughter, Becca, had to return to school in Mississippi to finish her semester and her presidency of Theta. She needed her life to keep moving forward. I wanted her to be *normal*. I thought it would help *me* return to *normal*.

Being in that house with Jackson, but in all other senses *alone*, was the darkest, saddest thing I've ever done in my life. I didn't know what to do.

What was I supposed to do?

Pictures of Helen sat piled all over the house, posters her friends had made, the flower blanket that had laid over her casket sat on my dining room table still and dying.

More of me died that night as I went to bed in that lonely bed. I just laid there, staring at the ceiling, wondering how I had come to that place. Jackson came to sleep in the bed with me, no doubt terrified of that tomb-like house himself.

Helen, you are our beautiful angel in Heaven. You can work miracles, too. Don't you want to see all of us together as a good loving family? Helen, I believe you have that capability to make it happen. I know you were angry. I pray that you and the angels and the blood of Jesus can change all that. I hope some solace for all of us can come from all this pain.

I really can't understand this chain of events. My heart can barely function. I'm missing my heart, you, so much.

I am your Mom, and Dad is your dad. We love you. Parts of us died when you did. Your dad is grieving in a different way than me.

Doug and I had a disconnect, and a wall grew between us too tall to ever climb. In our own ways, I'm sure we were both being selfish—too wrapped up in our own pain to help the other. I was scared I could never be what he needed, and too shattered to care.

Before long, it was clear I'd be spending the rest of my life without Doug. We sold our home and divorced. I worried constantly I wouldn't be able to make a stable home for Jackson during his remaining school years. I didn't want to miss any of his life. In the throes of my own drama with Doug, I felt I'd been making extra stress for Jackson, and I didn't want that for him. I felt so confused all the time. I *needed* him to live with me. I worried he would somehow forget me. Rebecca was out of college and off living a successful life.

Jackson was all I had left. I worried he'd lost faith in me.

Does he feel anxiety when he's with me? Am I irrelevant to him?

There was no patching my relationship with my husband and losing him meant losing so many things that make up a family. We'd have to juggle Jackson, both his welfare and his affections. I began to project the things that had happened to Helen on Jackson. I found myself praying for his friends to be a good influence on him. I prayed for any boy who entered his life to love and respect his mother.

Meanwhile, my heart was missing Helen.

If you truly love someone, you want them to be happy. I want Doug to be happy with or without me. If we aren't to be together, I pray you help us work through this as friends and parents of our children. I pray we show respect to each other. Please, Father, speak to both of our hearts. Help us fully understand Your plan and Accept Your Will. Speak to both of us in these hard times. Keep us both close to You. I pray Doug and I can find some peace with each other. We love each other and our family. For some reason that isn't enough. Please reveal our roadblock to both of us. Or simply show us how to move on, showing grace, and love and respect to the other.

Doug and I were together for twenty-seven years and we've known each other since I was six. Our families are best friends. We had decades of family trips and holidays together. When Doug and I had kids, both our parents were beyond thrilled.

Now it was all gone.

It was a difficult break up for me and I mourn our marriage still, if only because no one loved Helen more than we did, together. No one loves a child like the mother and the father do. It's a bond so strong only the other parent can understand. Her death is a pain only *we* can ever fully understand. Sometimes I want to share memories of Helen with Doug but he is unavailable for discussing our child. Other times, I feel he pretends she didn't exist and wishes to make all her memories disappear. This makes me sad and angry.

Life has been dealing me blow after blow.

Will it ever end?

PAIN

This chapter is a collection of my journal entries, thoughts and feelings over the five years following Helen's death so the reader can see how widely the emotional pendulum can swing. From the depths of despair to hope, from self-loathing to self-love, from fear to defiance—the death of a loved one can never be filtered into a straightforward emotional journey. Grief is not a straight line. It doesn't have any sort of a time frame. But there is beauty on the other side of so much pain. Beauty, and Love.

How does a mother's heart ever heal after losing one of her babies? I honestly don't believe mine ever will.

After Helen's death, I remember getting up every day and pretending I didn't want to go lay in that casket with her and die, too. She was my other half. I had no idea how to continue her successes. I couldn't ride Moonshine like she did. I could never be as brave as she was. All I knew how to do was love her with every ounce of my body, soul and mind.

Her presence had been larger than life. She loved animals. Her passion for riding always blew me away. She was never afraid. I knew she would grow up to be a veterinarian or some kind of healer of animals. How could I carry on her mission? How could I keep her alive? How could I keep her dreams going? There were so many questions...

Where did all her dreams go?

Where does all the love go?

Where do all of the tears flow?

Should I save them?

Maybe they're a secret potion that will allow me to talk to her or see her.

The imagination runs wild when you're desperate to *know* something. Death leaves so many questions and I wanted the answers, so constantly wrote and wrote hoping the answers would appear.

Slowly, I came to realize only time and surrendering to the unknown could produce the answers.

Helen left behind a standard poodle named Lily and I'd find myself imagining Lily's thoughts.

Where did my mommy go?

I knew she missed Helen. She'd *so* wanted to protect her. That terrible morning, Lily had curled beside Helen as her body grew cold. She wouldn't leave her side. I liked to imagine Lily saw a bright white light and watched the beautiful angels come to visit Helen. Maybe she watched Helen leave with them. Maybe Helen kissed Lily goodbye, and told her to watch over all the family and be her reminder to everyone. Helen would have told Lily she'd always be around and that she'd come lay with her and talk to her. Lily would be able to see her, and she could be there to let us know Helen was there beside us all, loving us and guiding us.

My mommy looks happy when she comes to visit me. She took me everywhere. She loves me and I love her, now and forever.

Believing Lily could still hear Helen's secrets, I held Lily close hoping Helen would eventually appear.

I am scared she can't hear me.

Waking up every day only to relive my baby girl Helen is gone is tearing me apart. I long to touch her. I want to hold her so tight and never let go. Trying to understand that my new normal is her not being here is the most difficult concept to grasp. I sit in her room and try to hear her laugh, praying I can feel her wrap her arms around me or that she will somehow speak to me. I want to believe Heaven is beautiful and that she is living with all the animals we've lost and loved.

Remember when Jewels drug you around the yard in your unicorn Halloween outfit?

I want to believe she's with Grandma Helen and she's protecting her, laughing with her, and that they are all watching over us. I like to think they're trying to tell me how much they love me and that they'll keep her safe.

God, I don't want to make you mad. I just want to

hold her. It sounds selfish. I know.
   She's my sweet love. She is my angel. She is my heart.

My Helen Jane! I was empty, and unsure I would ever feel alive again.

My torture came in many more forms than my agony over Helen's death. I was racked with guilt over not being more present for Jackson and Rebecca. I still had two children to care for—but all I wanted was my baby girl back so I could hold her and kiss her and hug her and smell her hair.

Helen, be with Jackson while he's having his tooth pulled. Tell him to suck it up and get over it! St. Michael Arch Angel, I pray for your intercession on behalf of me and Jackson and Becca and Doug. I ask that you armor us all today and every day to shield us. I command a hedge of protection around all of us, especially my precious Jackson. St. Michael, stand right beside him and guard him—his ears and eyes and heart. I pray love over Jackson. I pray he feels love and truth and that he wants to surround himself with like-minded kinds of people. Jackson deserves unconditional love and hugs and warmth and truth.

Jackson missed his sister and had a lot of questions. I prayed to Helen to hold him close and give him signs that she was with him. He tried so hard to be brave. He loved Helen but was afraid both she and I were mad because he was bored at her horse shows and didn't want to see Moonshine. He was so sweet. He'd say, "Mom, no star in the sky is more beautiful than Helen!"

I saw pieces of Helen in Jackson more and more each day and in the years following her death. He definitely has her smartass wit, infectious laugh, sarcastic tone, and thousand-megawatt smile. On February eighth, twenty-fourteen, Jackson's world had been turned upside down and sideways. I think he wanted to be just like her. I cried for him because he didn't get to see his big sister grow up and be his watchdog. I laughed because she didn't get to experience him being bigger and stronger than her so he could lock her in a closet...FINALLY! Through the years, I sometimes feared his pain over losing Helen would intensify, that each year, a new memory from that horrible day would surface and he'd relive it all over again. When he turned fifteen, he recalled watching as people carried his sister's body out of the house. That memory had taken four years to surface. Jackson is now seventeen, the same age Helen was when she died. I asked him on his birthday if it felt weird and he answered, "Not yet." One time, he said he forgot what she looked like and I swear my heart sank. I wanted to cry right then and there.

Forget? How could he forget?

These are the ways in which we heal and deal with trauma. Jackson will often say, "Helen is supposed to be here and watch over me and show me the ropes."

But we all know she's right beside him guiding him

along!

Helen, I know you are with me, I can feel you. You and Becca are my two angels. One angel in Heaven and the other is here on Earth. But once, you were both here. I am the luckiest mom in the world. Both my daughters are so amazingly smart and beautiful and kind and loving. I think both of you are so special and unique. Your qualities are superior to anything I have ever had. God at least gave me the strength and gift to raise both of you. It wasn't me. God has had his hand in all of it. I try every day to do my best with the talents he has given time. I love you, Helen.

I asked Helen to stay close to Becca and prayed she knew how much Helen loves her, even after death. Rebecca protected Helen and always wanted the best for her. No one was ever going to be good enough for her little sister. As I write this, Becca's wedding to Kyle is approaching and when Becca laments not having her sister there, I say, *believe me, Helen will be at the wedding.*

The bridal party is going to place flowers on the altar in Helen's memory. The boys will all have horseshoes on their lapels, and even her dad will be wearing a special horseshoe tie Rebecca picked out. Everyone is open to make any gesture that reminds them of Helen, because everyone had their own unique relationship with her.

Dear Helen, I am trying to empty my heart so I can hear you. I feel like you are talking to so many people close to me. Are you communicating to me with music? I feel you everywhere but I can't hear you. Every day I want to honor you in some way. My mind is on you, Helen Jane. I love you and miss you. I can't believe you were only with me for seventeen years. God has a plan I can't even begin to understand. You, Helen, are all knowing now. I don't know how to not miss you.

Today, I know I have so many tasks I need to do. I need to make lists like you did.

I started an inventory of my pain so I could address it best as I was able, though these inventories almost always turned into even more questions, prayers and wishes:

- The sadness is so deep. I am sad for the loss of Helen.
- Sad for the loss of my marriage and family.
- Sad that Jax and Becca lost their sister.
- Thank you God for all my circumstances. All of my worries. I am going always to tell You everything. But what will I do with the gifts and talents You have given me?
- What do I need to do today to keep my future life full?
- How do I get to where I can work?
- What talents will I need to develop?
- Help me to not complain to others.
- Help me to seek Your face and Your arms and Your love to guide me.

- Talking and writing to You helps me to be at peace helps me do just *today*.
- Fill my mind with Your Word from the bible.
- Fill my heart with kind and encouraging and loving words and thoughts and actions.
- I get scared of my future, so please help me to prepare.
- Am I getting stronger?
- Helen, am I getting closer to seeing you in my dreams?

Sometimes, I just have to sit and be quiet.

We are all in Palm Beach. I feel so much guilt. This isn't complete without you, so why aren't you here? My heart breaks every second. You were my light. I feel my light has gone out. I sit on a shelf and just watch the world going on around me. I want it to be Feb seventh—rewind—maybe all the events will change. I love you; I want you here.

My body doesn't feel whole. I look in the mirror and only see one side of me. Helen, you and I were almost like one person.

I could see you swimming out in the water this morning. I want you to be here. I miss you. My heart is still shattered. It can't be fixed. I cherish all my pics and videos. I love you to the moon and back. My love for you grows stronger every day. Come back, please. God, please, why can't I have my baby here?

I still cry when I think of Helen. I laugh when I think of her. I can even get mad, thinking about her as a teenager. I always feel the deepest love. I carry her everywhere with me. I gave birth to her—of course, I feel her every move. When I am not doing my grief work or keeping busy, I get scared I can't feel her, as if she isn't reachable. I get mad at myself. I should be compassionate with myself. I am working on that.

I remember her life and every second of when she was here walking on Earth. I wish I could remember everything since her death but I really can't. Maybe I am blocked or maybe it's God's protection over me.

I talk to Helen. I see her in my head and in pictures. I hear her voice when I have conversations with her in my head or out loud—I'm not always sure which. I will be anywhere on vacation or home or busy with a project and I can burst into tears. It doesn't matter the hour or what's going on around me. I cry or I go inside myself to a place of emptiness. I see everything going on around me. Sometimes, I even have conversations, laughing, but I'm not really there. Only my physical body is there. How does this happen? What takes place in these moments? Sometimes, it goes on for days and days. I don't know.

I search my mind for solace. I pray. I want to meditate, but often I feel frustrated. I want it to come easily to me. I want to write every feeling and thought and sometimes I feel the need to log my *lack* of feeling. The numbness. I want to describe it. I need people around me to understand, but they won't. They can't. I find that sometimes I don't want to burden other people. These people love me and want to support me and be there for me. I never mean to push people away.

Why would anyone care about my day-to-day world of emotion?

I see pictures of me and I feel like I don't know me. Maybe I don't want to know me anymore, this new version of me without Helen.

Missing my daughter and trying each day to pick myself up and be 'normal' is the hardest thing. To live productively and be happy and engage in relationships sometimes feels too much. I do know God and the Guardian Angels never leave my side. I can feel their strength. I believe they want me to pick each foot up and move forward day to day.

Even with my faith, it gets lonely. I get lost in my thoughts of her. I go to places in my mind that I create to visualize her, as if she's alive and doing what I think she would be doing at this age.

Traveling to other countries and being around people who don't know me or ever knew Helen sometimes gives me relief. I constantly want to be away. Through travel mourners can escape without using substances, but still, my grief counselor says this is not the healthiest way to process my grief. I don't drink to excess or do drugs to try and deal with my life without Helen here on Earth. My distraction is travel—I get on a plane and maybe I can feel *something* new and hopeful. Just feeling the sun on my skin, or riding on a boat, the salt drying on my skin, can make me forget for a moment.

Relationships are difficult. I can get quiet, pull away, sink into my shell and not want to talk. I feel I can't be what the other person may need or want from a relationship. It's not fair to them. Yet, I crave companionship and touch. I dream of having someone in my life who wants to love me—the after-Helen me. The person I haven't even learned to love yet.

I'm no longer the same as before. Parts of me are put away neatly in a box, because opening that box could take me to a darkness from which I can't return. The dark places are scary, but then there are holidays and her birthday and angel day—I feel numb a lot of those times. I can exercise very intensely and just keep my head down to get through it.

Sometimes the pain inside my heart makes me nauseous and I just want to hide. Friends don't ask me to do many things anymore—I'm sure because I started saying no to lots of big gatherings and groups. I don't know how to have conversations about their kids and lives and hear about how everyone else's life has throttled on.

I'm trying to find my way and deal with the death of a child and a 26-year marriage all at the same time. I am doing my best. I have hope and faith every day. I have a beautiful life with Rebecca and Jackson. I don't have a bad attitude—I think positively and say lots of prayers, but it is still a struggle to fully function and get on with my life. God never said it would be easy and that life would be roses all the time, but I know he said He would see me through it. I keep the faith and hope for a better tomorrow. Inside my mind and heart, I can still have pain *and* be joyful. I can cry and miss her and talk to her and spiritually hug her. I can also find happiness in a small walk in the park. Pain and joy can be felt all at once.

Getting to the emotions, their nooks and crannies, is helping me to get closer to Helen.

Still, my soul never feels fully at rest.

HAVING FAITH

Lord, I want to be like the one to whom you said, "Woman, you have great faith! Your request is granted!" Matthew 15:28 God, please flourish this kind of faith in me!

I am grateful for the seventeen years I had with Helen here on Earth. Thankful for all the blessings of these three children that God has brought into my life. Helen's death is hard for me to deal with, but I know she's at peace and that she is doing God's work every day. I fully rely on God's strength and I have faith and hope in his will for my life.

My help comes from the Lord, who made Heaven and Earth. ~ Psalm 121:2

My faith helps me daily with my pain. I know God sees me hurting, and He has a purpose for this. I live by Faith and not by sight. What is happening here on Earth, my pain, and my sadness are temporary. Heaven is eternal; I will see Helen again and we will never be apart! I also know He and Helen know the full picture and I have to trust in His plan. I do find comfort every day knowing she is safe with Jesus and our blessed mother, Mary, and that is very comforting. My heart can rejoice!

Lord give me strength to get thru this day. Grant me peace and humility and grace and kindness and discernment. Heavenly Father, I want to sharpen my skills and the tools that you have given me. I feel I am here to do something to help others to make a difference. Lord, put me on the path to sharpen my skills you want to use for the greater good. I want to do Your will. I'm going to let you show me what to do. Put the right people in my path and reveal to me how to find them.

Fill me with your love and I pray you heal me back to a better Jammie.

Sometimes, I like to imagine what it will be like when I'm with Helen in Heaven. I envisioned thousands of angels wearing beautiful white gowns with gold adornments, playing games above my head. I see Helen's perfect curls cascading down her  back as she dances among them with laughter.

I can't wait to spend eternity with you. I can braid your hair and we can have many talks together and ride horses together and celebrate together. My beautiful Helen, you went to sleep and left us. I can't argue with God but I want to. It's so painful to wake up each day without you here. I need to know that you hear me and that you hug me and that you want to see me too. Can you? Are you and Grandma Helen sharing stories? Are all of you missing us? Can Lily see you?

The first Christmas without Helen left my mind scattered with thoughts, feelings and emotions I couldn't allow to rise to the surface for fear I might drown beneath the weight of them. I went to Holy Redeemer for mass with my family and listened to Bishop Rice as best I could. He asked us to promise to visit the baby Jesus in the manger and give him our hearts. That was all he wanted from us during that holiday season.

When mass was over I moved to the nativity scene and I gave Jesus my heart, but as I knelt there before Him, I found my gaze drawn to Mary, there by the infant's side, watching over Him. I realized I had something in common with Mary I hadn't before Helen's death.

We had both lost a child.

For the first time, I truly felt the pain of her loss. Both of us had been given amazing gifts, but God needed them back to fulfill His purpose.

Blessed Mother, enfold me in your arms. Kiss my tears

away. You know the pain of losing a child. Heal me enough to where I can keep loving and supporting my other kids and give myself fully to them. I want Helen to myself. I want to be with her in my dreams and spend my days talking to her. Please help me extend my love to others. I need Helen to know every day that I love her.

God has put me here for a reason.

HEALING

When you're hurting from a loss like mine, you'll try anything to make the pain go away. For me, every day is a balance between keeping busy to *avoid* thinking about losing Helen, and working to process my emotions and heal.

I was going to have to face my pain and find a way to cope. I couldn't roll into a ball and die, as much as I sometimes wanted to. I had other children. I had my own life. I had to go on.

But how? How do you go on when it feels like your heart is being torn from your chest every time your lost child's dog looks at you? Every time you see her face in someone else's? Every time you hear a laugh and you turn to find it isn't her?

Many people turn to alcohol and other substances to dull the ache—and I certainly considered that option myself. It seemed easier than finding a way to work through my agony. However, it didn't take long to realize dulling the pain with alcohol one evening only made the next day ten times worse. My anxiety would reach new highs.

Numbing my brain wasn't the answer.

So, I resolved to try *everything*. I resolved to remain open to every possible support and treatment. I had an amazing grief counselor who literally held my hand daily and slowly brought me back to some sort of place of actually feeling. I had received many daily devotional books from people who loved and cared about me. How blessed was I to have been surrounded by so much love?

I couldn't feel it at that time.

I used to think, *someone could light me on fire and I wouldn't even feel it.* I think back to those dark and lonely nights full of tears and insomnia, and how afraid I was of daylight coming the next day, the next, the next...*and still not having Helen.* Every morning, after maybe three hours of sleep, I would wake up and double over in pain and clutch my chest and wonder where my heart had gone. What dark beast had come and ripped it mercilessly from my chest? And *why?* I felt hollow and cold and the emptiness was so vast I didn't even feel at home in my own body anymore. For many days and months I watched myself from outside my body.

Who is this person moving me all around?

I was sure I was dead, too. I watched myself go from day-to-day, task-to-task, trying to connect and be present.

Thank the Heavenly Father above for stepping in and taking over!

Jackson needed his mother!

I would look into his big blue eyes, wanting to say, *I have the answers.* But I didn't. I just hugged him and prayed we would survive the hell into which we'd been thrown. Jackson, Rebecca and I went to the grief counselor together to help us deal with the overwhelming sadness of losing Helen, the force of nature who'd ruled our worlds for seventeen years. She was a force we laughed with, yelled at, and fought with, but, *my goodness,* she was such a big piece of each of us we felt we were missing parts of our bodies without her. My three children are so different, but also so very similar. There are little, shiny, golden threads weaving through the three of them, making up a glorious and exquisite tapestry.

What happens when one of those threads comes loose?

It wants to unravel slowly, but I was *not* going to let that happen to those of us who remained, and neither was Helen!

I went to an intuitive healer, one who combined her services with healing massage, in the hopes of releasing the emotions trapped in my body. Through her, I believe I've met with Helen. Over time, I became more and more receptive to my connection to Helen, and now I don't even need the assistance of a healer—I connect with her without an earthly go-between. We have conversations and I can hear her always encouraging me. The most beautiful experiences would happen when I was traveling near any kind of water. I could see Helen in the distance watching me. She was wearing a white linen flowing dress and her curls were always flowing behind her in the wind, free....like she is now! Free from pain or hurt from her time here on Earth.

When I hear her, Helen tells me her death isn't my fault. I can hear her as clearly as if she is sitting beside me.

"Mom, it's no one's fault. It was a careless mistake. You've got to live your life. No one loved me more than you did. It wasn't my intention. As much as you miss me, I miss you—but it isn't your fault."

I think Helen is still with us. At first, I could smell her familiar smell. That was easy. Now I see her. Interestingly, she looks the same to me as she does to my daughter Rebecca when *she* sees her. We see Helen at fifteen or sixteen—she has a certain look about her that places her at that age for us. There's something about the way she wore her hair then that's different from how she wore it at the time of her death. I'm not sure I can even put my finger on what it is exactly.

How strange we can both see her younger than she was when she died!

Does Helen really visit us? It's hard not to think she does. I can tell you her playful nature didn't change after death. My neighbor, who was close to her, says my daughter's antics and the tricks she'd play when she was alive still happen around her house.

She also moves my and Jackson's stuff. When I'm driving, sometimes the radio stations will change and a song special to us will come on the radio. I can sense her energy and I know she's trying to communicate with me.

She hides things from me and leaves the most precious presents, like when I found her horseshoe necklace in a spot I'd already looked. There are days I can't wait to see what gifts she leaves for me. I've asked her to give me the gift of more leg muscle for riding—though that might have been beyond her scope! I've also asked her to share her bravery with me.

I might be getting greedy. Ha!

I can feel her pull my attention towards beauty. I notice the flowers and the palms and the sparkling water. I see the rainbows she made for me to see. Certain birds and always dragonflies send the message of Helen. Maybe she'll leave me a treasure under a piece of coral, or she'll guide me to a spot she loved and we'll enjoy the beauty.

The gifts are always special and I know they're just for me.

My beautiful Helen – I saw you today when I was sitting down by the water after I swam. Why haven't you visited me in my dreams? Can you send me messages or thoughts? I keep waiting for you to appear. I want you to come into my room and wrap your arms around me and tell me it wasn't real. It's so weird to say, but I will be so happy and ready for my death. I can't wait to see you again and have eternity with you. Bishop Rice said, "You see what you believe. You are living what you believe."

Do you ever wish you had chosen to stay here with us?

Did you see all the kids today? Their adventure into Fernandez? I know you would have been the first one to jump in!

I've also explored Eye Movement Desensitization and Reprocessing (EMDR), which is a therapy often used for victims of post-traumatic stress disorder. While people associate PTSD with soldiers, the death of a loved one causes many of the same symptoms. During this therapy, patients relive traumatic or trigger experiences (seeing Helen's body in the mortuary, for example) while directing eye movements in particular ways. The idea is to divert yourself while you remember, which makes the remembering less stressful. Over time, training yourself to replace the traumatic events with new happier mental images helps lessen the impact of the memory.

Learning techniques for remembering painful events was an important step. Since losing Helen, I've had to turn inward and face the dark corners where I suffer guilt. It's beyond painful. A heaviness comes upon me, and I feel as if I'm trying to drag a dense, black hole of emotions with me. My heart hurts and my mind goes places that are too scary and lonely to describe.

I missed all the signs.

I pretended it was all okay. I believed Helen was *not* an addict. I discussed rehab, but didn't act quickly enough.

Could I have saved her from taking those drugs?

I don't know.

I don't think so.

Helen seemed to know she was going to die. I don't think she killed herself, but I believe she had a choice and she chose to leave this Earth. Why, I'll never know or understand.

I don't sit around trying to figure out why. God will reveal all those answers when I die and I go to Heaven. I've learned that love endures all things. Love knows no boundaries or limits when it comes to our children. I've learned that the depth of joy, happiness and fulfillment your kids bring into your life is the greatest gift of all. We parents forget our children really belong to God. We're just lucky enough to be chosen to care for them and love them for as long as He lets us.

How have I gotten this far? Holidays come and go, Christmases, birthdays and a junior ring ceremony where her father and I went up and accepted her ring. Only my spiritual strength enabled me to walk on stage in front of two hundred-plus people and collect her ring. I also felt compelled to speak at her graduation. All of these beautiful girls made me feel alive. They all loved Helen and I wanted to share my gratitude with them. Angels carried me, I'm sure of it. It had to be God's grace, love and unconditional love. Not my own strength—Heavens no! Many days, my earthly body doesn't even want to move. Sometimes, I feel dead washing over me.

Not a single mile-marker has felt right or okay on any level, but something moves me through.

It's Christmas 2014. I can't fully feel the sadness of Helen not being here with us. I'm sitting here typing and I can see you, Helen Jane, and I can feel your presence. I know you are here with us, and I am comforted knowing that you are safe in Heaven and not here on Earth where even more pain could have hurt you. I have to believe that you are close to the four of us right now, so we can get through today and tomorrow... and every day since you went to Heaven.

For two years, I couldn't spend the holidays with my family the way I had. As the children, cousins and family gathered, all I could see was Helen *not* there. Every group of giggling children was just a group of people *without Helen*. In her place stood my own darkness and anger. Emptiness.

I mentally made lists of the things I couldn't change and then things I knew were true.

- Helen isn't coming back... but she is safe.
- Doug is never coming back. He will find his own way to work through his grief, in a

world where men aren't supposed to show weakness.

- Becca, Jax and I are a family and we have our future together.

When I wasn't making lists, I was saying tiny prayers for strength, clarity and hope. I would just keep repeating scripture; I still do when my mind drifts to missing her. My world had become a complicated tangle of feelings and new emotions and disappointments. Listing them helped me face them head-on.

- Please help me to not let what others think of me define me.
- Let my children love me and their father.
- Keep my heart on the healing process.
- Help fill me with grace, love, understanding and generosity.
- Open my heart, open my mind, but let in only what's from You.
- Protect me from evil.

I am accepting my adversity. I offer it up to you, Father, for your purpose for me. My suffering does have meaning. I trust in your plan each day I am thankful for all the hidden blessings. Every day, I get to drive Jackson to school and teach him how to make puppy chow, and I help him with homework or we just sit idly together. I find joy in the day-to-day tasks and the small things, like a beautiful sunrise or the full moon. This shows me there is light from the darkness. A sunrise fills me with hope and a future. I see Helen's light in the sunrise. Now a sunrise means a new day and a new opportunity to live this beautiful life God has put before me. Another day to watch Jackson grow and hug him tight. Kiss his sweet face. To encourage him to be the best that he can be. To teach him to help others and always to remember to be kind to his peers and others because we don't know what battles they are facing.

My diary entries, like my thoughts, aren't always filled with pain and sadness. Sometimes, they're silly, goofy, and my own playfulness reminds me of the joy Helen brought on Earth and still brings to me when I remember her.

A typical morning in Heaven: God is drinking his coffee and all the angels are gathering to share stories of their busy evenings tending to their humans on Earth. God is listening to prayer requests.

I also find solace by completing silly goals and tasks I'd hoped to do with Helen. Though the gestures are simple, it brings me closer to her in a happy, fulfilling way. For instance, my daughters and I had planned to purchase matching bracelets. Rebecca and I went ahead and did this, and had them monogrammed with *HJF Forever.*

The man who sold the bracelets to us was named Francis—just like Helen's patron Saint, St Francis of Assis. What were the chances? Becca and I couldn't get over it. It was as if Helen wanted to let us know she was with us. As if she led us to *that* store to be sure we knew.

Listing actions and thoughts also helps me focus on the things I know will help my healing.

- Let peace come first. Then proceed. The task will get done naturally and on time.
- I will trust that I will receive all I need to get me through today.
- It is okay to allow ourselves to cocoon during times of transformation. We can surrender to the process and trust that a new exciting energy is being created within us. Before long we will take new wings and fly.
- Today, I will be open to new awareness about the areas where I need healthier boundaries.
- Strive for an attitude of financial responsibility in thought and action. Ask for Divine Wisdom. Listen to God's leadings.
- What is the dream my heart desires?
- It's hard to put my children's dreams after my own. I think of how I can help them achieve theirs.
- I want to grow my roots with my family and share holidays and all occasions with them.
- I want to write a book about the journey of losing a child, grieving and coming out the

other side stronger and more aware and appreciative.

- I want to speak to other parents who are grieving. Learn from them, too.
- I want to share Helen's story and honor her memory.
- Be close to my children through solid communicative relationships. Share in their future lives continuing to love them unconditionally.
- Love myself and continue to do things for myself that spiritually help me grow.
- Trust that closing a relationship will open me up to all good things that are coming my way.
- Receive love and help from others.
- Have self-respect.

AND NEVER EVER LET A DAY GO BY WITHOUT LAUGHING WITH MY GIRL!

Sometimes, just a short poem, cribbed in the corners of my journal, can make me feel better.

She was born to me but she wanted to run wild and be free.

The world around could not tame her. Had they tried, boy, what a mess that would have been!

~~~

She looked beautifully out of place, like the moon during the day.

Her eyes danced like the moon's reflection on the water at night.

She now resides in my soul, healing the hidden pain.

Lovingly holding me and whispering, "It's OK!"

As I rest inside her wings, she nods and says, "Mom, you are going to be alright!"

~~~

Helen's eyes sparkle like sapphires
Her curls flow with the wind
The way in which she melted your heart with just her smile and a grin.
Her love for you embraced
Your heart was wild as a fire
She will always be with our soul until the end.

~~~

Stars light up the night sky, I see you dancing among them.
The stars are diamonds and you make them shine
The light in your eyes, the gorgeous sea of blue, they speak to me, they shine for me, and take me to our special place.
Our special place is the place only you and I know.
We sit and talk and I hold your hand and you tell me you love me and I say I love you more.
The conversations and times only we shared—I treasure them ever so deeply in the depths of my soul. I will never tell our secrets. I will forever call you mine.

The stairs to Heaven I can't wait to see, because their presence will mean I'm closer to seeing you.

In the years since Helen's passing, I've taken steps forward and steps back. Grief is not a straight line. It twists and turns to dead ends and we back up and try again.

On January first, twenty-nineteen, Lily, Helen's standard poodle, died and it was like losing her all over again. Lily was a living, furry bridge from me to Helen, and losing her was devastating.

One step forward. One step back. One step forward again. Sometimes, a few.

At some point you have to count on yourself. You can't always count on your dog to be there. You can't always count on others to help you through your bad moments. So many people were at the funeral lending me their strength, but then they were gone. It isn't their responsibility to be there for us for the rest of our lives. As Helen's family, we're the ones forced to carry the burden of our grief for longer and with more intensity than family, friends or work acquaintances will ever do.

After the funeral, so as not to be a burden to these friends who have done their best to support me, I joined a grieving mom's Facebook group, A Bed for My Heart. (https://www.facebook.com/ABedForMyHeart)

These became the people who were there for

me, day after day, when I needed to share with someone who understood my particular pain.

But I believe you don't have to lose a child to learn from another person's loss. Years later, many of the people at the funeral still tell me not a day goes by they don't think about Helen. Maybe they're only trying to make me feel better, but I do believe she lives on in each and every one of us. She taught us how to live life to the fullest. I had people write me letters after the funeral—people I didn't even know—telling me how the funeral changed their lives and how they want to *live*.

THE UNIVERSE HAS MY BACK – LESSONS I'VE LEARNED

I can do the impossible because I have been through the unimaginable.

Say, *I love you*.
Losing a child has taught me to say *I love you* to *all* the people I love as often as possible. Love lives deep inside the heart. It lifts us up and carries us and shoulders our hurts and disappointments. Appreciate and hold onto this kind of love.

Hugs are healing.
I hug everyone tightly, even if it's someone I just met. Touch can heal wounds deep in a person's soul.

Smiles for complete strangers can change their life.

Making eye contact with other humans as you walk down a street can help people feel acknowledged and change their attitude in an instant. Day-to-day life consumes humans. We go from one project to the next, walk from here to there. We come in contact with so many other human beings through the course of the day, never knowing some of these people are struggling with depression, sadness, stress, unhappiness. Being gracious and offering a smile can save a life. Help someone feel acknowledged. Receiving a smile opens lines of communication. Sometimes just a kind word from a stranger has transformed me and helped me heal.

Remember not all grief is sad.

I often find myself thinking of Helen's crazy antics here on Earth, like the time she put a service vest on Lily and took her to the mall, and I belly laughed.

I remember how we laughed at

movies (cried during *Spirit*), how she hated *Desperate Housewives* and loved *Greys Anatomy,* and how we watched every episode of *Bates Motel* together. I think about little things that seemed unimportant at the time, like how I made her a smoothie every day of her last year—banana, cocoa powder, ice, almond milk and peanut butter. I remember all the silly games we played and the tricks we pulled on each other, and it makes me see beauty in my world in every place I shared with her. The beauty and joy she left behind is everywhere.

I still have tears, but even during the most intense moments of my grief when I miss her infectious energy, I will sometimes burst out laughing.

Love doesn't understand time or distance.

Helen could take me from zero to one hundred in two seconds. That didn't change after her death.

Men and women grieve very differently.

I've learned to let people grieve *their* way. At first, I found myself judging people, believing if they didn't grieve the same way I did, it meant they'd forgotten about Helen. I know now everyone grieves in their own way. While Doug's style of grief left little room for us as a couple, he could only do it the way that felt right to him. He had to do what he needed to push through.

Lean on your faith.

I've learned how strong my faith is, and how bold other people's faith can be as well. I've learned receiving prayers and love from others, even strangers, can help a human put one foot in front of the other. Prayers and love from family, friends, people from parishes and schools have carried me through the darkest days.

Your heart can be crushed into a billion pieces and still keep beating.

Even though the calendar days keep rolling and the years go by, the day your child receives their angel wings is the day your body splits. Sometimes it's like watching myself from outside my body. I see part of me missing when I look in the mirror. But I'm alive and living my life. Sometimes, I don't know what computer chip was inside me that helped me to keep moving through the worst moments, but it kept ticking.

Cherish your memories, but be in the present moment to create new ones.

Every memory, be it good or bad, is important. Thanks to my memories and photos, Helen can still make me smile. I can hear her laugh and smell her smell. Now, I continue making memories with all my loved ones. Take lots of pictures. No death can take away your memories and experiences.

I am strong and brave, but also weak and vulnerable.

It's okay to be strong *and* weak. We can't be strong every day. Some days, I want to be alone with my own memories of Helen and cry, laugh, get mad and then release it. For so long, I felt I wasn't allowed to admit how hard it is not having her here on Earth anymore.

A NOTE ON THE OPIOID EPIDEMIC

I fully trust in God. Helen, today, I went to the chapel and literally pretended I was pulling my heart out of my chest and laid it on the altar. I forget you can probably see me.

I miss you every second, Helen. I promise I'm going to be active in my life. I want to reach parents and kids and help them. I don't want other families to hurt like you hurt. I will keep getting help to make me a better mom.

Helen's friends don't want other people to lose a friend like they did. It doesn't need to happen. Opioids don't have to be the epidemic they've become. The medical companies say opioids aren't addictive.

They've been lying.

The corruption and greed that has created the opioid problem is overwhelming.

In Missouri, where my daughter died, there is no prescription plan mandate program. It is the only state that doesn't have a database tasked with tracking prescriptions from county to county and state to state. That database, in other states, is the only thing stopping people from going to five doctors, one after the next, getting Xanax prescriptions at each one, for example. When it is so easy for people to hoard drugs, it's no wonder why Helen found drugs readily available.

Why is Missouri the only state without a prescription plan mandate? Because one senator in southern Missouri fought to keep it that way. He says it is an 'invasion of privacy' to keep prescription information on patients.

In 2017, they held a Prescription Drug Monitoring Program (PDMP) senate committee with twenty senators on it to address the issue. Holly Rehder, the District 148 Republican senator trying to fight against the blocking of the database, heard about my story through a friend of ours who lost his son through overdose. This friend, Gary, went to college with my sister, but he lived in Kansas, so he couldn't testify on behalf of Missouri for Holly. He contacted me and asked if I'd go to the Missouri senate committee. I said, *sure.* The tragedy of Helen's death had laser-locked my focus on the opioid epidemic. The lies and greed I'd been reading about already had my blood boiling.

Gary shared with me even more facts and numbers on how many deaths had occurred, and I agreed to give a personal account of what happened to Helen. There were many others there sharing their stories of loss, including another senator whose best friend had lost a child, but in the end, the bill was defeated.

Missouri still doesn't have a PDMP. Missouri needs a PDMP set in place now. Why? Because this alarming escalation in loss of life and complete devastation to surviving families is out of control. Painful and unnecessary.

Nobody is doing anything.

We tried to keep the momentum going, and I participated in some interviews after the senate hearing. Josh Hawley, Missouri's Attorney General, announced he was tired of big pharmaceutical companies making billions of dollars by flooding our streets with opioids and then lying about the drugs' addictive effect. He filed the largest lawsuit in Missouri history to make the pharma companies pay. Since then, multiple states have followed his lead, banding together to hold Big Pharma accountable. He asked me to tell my story with some other people in July 2017. Talking in front of news cameras was more intimidating than speaking in front of the senate committee, and soon I saw myself speaking on Fox News with Brett Baier and to all the big newspapers. And though our only goal was to change minds and the policy in the hopes it would save lives, I still faced my share of negative feedback. Any time you're in the public eye, someone will have a problem with what you're saying. It was insane. In my speech, I said the opioid epidemic had no class or color, that it would take anyone, and some people still complained my words were just another example of white privilege.

I wouldn't wish the privilege of having your daughter's life stolen on anyone.

I drowned out the negative comments. I did the interviews and got the word out there as best I could until the campaign had simply run its cycle and the press lost interest.

I'm still willing to talk to senators but it is hard, because for the most party, our elected officials really don't care how opioids are tearing apart our families. Though Missouri still had their campaign to get the PDMP, in 2018 I moved to Florida, so I became less helpful to them as an example of what opioids could do to a Missouri child. Politicians and other people get too much money from Big Pharma, so no matter how many people fight to fix the problem, there are others fighting on the other side and it all ends in deadlock. Big Pharma should be paying for rehab centers to help people end the addition they claim doesn't exist, but any attempts to make them accountable gets squashed. New Jersey's Governor Christie was one politician who made real headway. He was implementing programs, building facilities and helping people get rehab. Then other scandals took him off the radar.

I haven't even seen public service announcements about opioids. Have you? I've seen them about bullying and even littering, but nothing about an epidemic that killed over forty-two thousand in 2016 and over seventy thousand in 2017. Opioid deaths are trending upward at a terrifying pace.

Groups like Shatterproof are small beacons of hope. Shatterproof's Substance Use Disorder Treatment Task Force has developed the National Principles of Care, a standard for addiction treatment based on proven research. Sixteen leading healthcare payers have agreed to unite around this standard pulling Shatterproof closer to ensuring every American with a substance use disorder has access to quality, evidence-based treatment.

Shatterproof also takes on federal and state advocacy battles, mobilizing families affected by addiction and providing them with a platform to make their voices heard. They've helped fifteen states pass life-saving legislation, broadened access to lifesaving naloxone, strengthened prescription-drug-monitoring programs, and ensured prescriber practices align with CDC guidance on opioids.

By joining forces with advocacy groups across the country, they've supported federal laws like the Comprehensive Addiction and Recovery Act (CARA) and the 21st Century Cures Act. They also advocate to protect insurance coverage for substance use disorders, joining the federal health care fight whenever the issue is raised. To shatter the deadly stigma of addiction, they've built a Community Alliance program with nearly five hundred local ambassadors, providing education and supporting advocacy efforts.

Shatterproof's founder and CEO, Gary

Mendell, lost his son to addition and realized very quickly politicians weren't going to solve the problem. He understood that, to individual families and addicts, it was all about finding a source of strength. It was about getting people help.

It's insane to me that the pharmaceutical companies bear no responsibility for the epidemic they've caused. They should be building facilities and funding them. They created the problem and they should be fixing it. It's frustrating.

Purdue Pharma, the maker of Oxycontin, agreed to pay Oklahoma $270 million to avoid facing trial over misleading marketing practices and misrepresentation. More states planned to sue, so Purdue Pharma then filed bankruptcy as part of a $10 billion agreement.

They still deny any wrongdoing.

Funny, I can't remember the last time I went bankrupt trying to pay someone for things that weren't my fault.

Oxycontin is just the tip of the iceberg. One of my niece's best friends overdosed after Helen's death. She looked it up online, made herself a deadly drug cocktail and wrote a letter she wanted to end her life. Kids are eating "Xanny bars," named after the bar-like shape of Xanax pills, to avoid drinking their calories. One of Helen's friends has acted out in so many ways I fear she's headed down the same path. Another friend's child has been hooked on heroin. I have a nephew, the last one to talk to Helen, who's struggled with cocaine.

Didn't you see your cousin die?

Since Helen's death, her friends have had four or five other kids in their circle die from an overdose.

Tens of thousands of our sons, daughters and loved ones die every year as a consequence of prescription opioid and heroin use. According to the US Center for Disease Control and Prevention, this is "the worst drug overdose epidemic in US history." This epidemic reaches across all demographics. Today, it's estimated that 4.5

million people in the U.S. are addicted to prescription opioids and 467,000 to heroin. My seventeen-year-old daughter is a part of that statistic.

How many parents and other loving family members does it take to stand together, broken devastated and shattered, to get the government to pass the bills necessary to help these addicts and their families? Too many legislators think it's a back-alley problem, but there are too many pills on the street.

As a society, we're doing something wrong.

THE END

You can read more about Jammie Fabick and dealing with loss at http://JammieFabick.com

ABOUT THE AUTHOR

Jammie Fabick is a philanthropist, multi-million-dollar investor and author of *Gaining An Angel,* where she shares the never-ending journey that is grieving the loss of a child. As an activist and mother of three, she has spoken alongside Missouri Attorney General Josh Hawley at news conferences throughout the mid-west and has been featured on Fox News, *The Washington Post, Chicago Tribune,* CBS News and AP News, speaking against the opioid epidemic sweeping the United States.

Jammie continues to share her messy truth

about grief, divorce, betrayal and her continued journey to re-building a more authentic life. She lives in Florida with her son and two poodles.

Made in the USA
Monee, IL
27 May 2022